Threat Come Close

Threat Come Close

Aaron Coleman

Four Way Books
Tribeca

Please direct all inquiries to:
Editorial Office
Four Way Books
POB 535, Village Station
New York, NY 10014
www.fourwaybooks.com

Library of Congress Cataloging-in-Publication Data

Names: Coleman, Aaron, author.
Title: Threat come close / Aaron Coleman.
Description: New York, NY : Four Way Books, [2018] | Includes bibliographical
references.
Identifiers: LCCN 2017029356 | ISBN 9781945588044 (softcover : acid-free
paper)
Classification: LCC PS3603.O4324 A6 2018 | DDC 811/.6--dc23
LC record available at https://lccn.loc.gov/2017029356

This book is manufactured in the United States of America and printed on acid-free paper.

Four Way Books is a not-for-profit literary press. We are grateful for the assistance
we receive from individual donors, public arts agencies, and private foundations.

PROUD MEMBER

[clmp]

We are a proud member of the Community of Literary Magazines and Presses.

Distributed by University Press of New England
One Court Street, Lebanon, NH 03766

For our Colemans and our Wards,
our Jacksons and our Fords . . .

Contents

3 : of sudden roots

4 : risk a bridge

Notes

"You people think you're free."

Very Many Hands

You remind me of the Underground Railroad. I've learned to watch for the kerosene lamp aglare in your distance. Past the fuel and wick at the far end of your forest, there's a mud basement, a soot-slick coal cellar with my sleeping body's name on it. I could lie still forever in that part of you. But then I'd never make it North.

***

I am made of what I am afraid to remember. Come tell me more about what I was—about the brothers, mind-ancient now, fleeing Mississippi with spilled moon ready in their eyes. Go back and tell me about that one before that one that sold a mother. Wait. Then give me more about the buzz of war, of San Diego shipyards, of handsome sailors you couldn't trust. Make vivid the night with me before me in it. Tell me what was lost on the way to Detroit. Tell me what was lost leaving Detroit. Tell me why I'm afraid for and of Detroit. Tell me Desire can't mean what it meant anymore. And I can't mean what I meant anymore. Am I lovesick with amnesia or nostalgia?

1
we weren't safe

St. Inside and Not

Being tornado, being wind-stuck,
Being swamp-swallowed and forgotten, being
Gangster-gone-ghost. Being leaking
And prohibited. Being rugged
Smirk and gut exposed, stone church
Roof removed, ivy-spindled throat. Being
Forever-far from coasts. Being echo clang and
Shale-sick grease rag. Being trundled down
The conveyor belt, the wound wound river being
Time-tight, squeezing and seething
And flooding. Being burnheart and holy
Jelly Roll squall and squalor and
Ma called squaw battered in missing shame-
Laden eyes. Being missed and called family, anchor,
Last name: Gone. Being turned into translation,
Being altar, being mother praying *God save
Me* in a language I'll never know. Being hands
Held high above head, body blown open. Being
Bit-nickel never trusted, being
Runaway sharecropper castrated, burned
Away in pieces in hand-licked heavy
Envelopes. Being letters scrawled: *you
Missed a big, fiery one. Wish you were
Here.* Being midnight ripped

Off the face of constellation. Being
Rage shattered in the body, before
Each risk I live, let die, follow.

On Forgiveness

I am a half question seeping into cracked ice
      leaning over the bar's worn wood. Fear
weighted with ache, anxious in the fleshed
      angles of two faces. Slurred symmetry in me
and my old man's shadow when he cackles.
      Saliva and vodka flick embers working
fire into my skin. No one else sees the sway
      and lean in his bulk, the terror coarse
in his veins. His loose hands hold slick,
      wet glass; a promise of sharpness. Don't
murmur *I love you,* this time. Don't
      come close. Give me the keys and shut
the fuck up if I swerve in the dark
      summer heat by the swamp
land you taught me to own.

Viciousness in Ends

blood and trust   in my mouth
on the ground   sweltering each
swing harder   dizzy still   to protect what?

inside red and black gloves with quarter-
worn knuckles   part of a man   two fists thick
no way to know the stranger   from my

brother's hand – the boxing glove still hot
past it sticky   hand slipping into –
we refused to go   the fear in our throats –

stuck like meat in our teeth   *and it was good*   and it was
from one another   and sweat genesis   and took
uncut grass   we laughed   face down

in the yellow   to press each other's necks   like dull blades
and used our forearms – where he breaks
we laughed   because we swore   a man is born

into each other's sharp backs   point blank
we shot the metal bb's   we shot
the metal bb's point blank into each other's

sharp backs   because we swore a man is born

where he breaks   we laughed and used

    our forearms like dull blades   to press each other's

necks face down   in the yellow uncut grass   we laughed

    and sweat genesis and took   from one another

and it was good   and it was stuck   like meat

in our teeth the fear   in our throats – we refused

    to go past it   sticky hand slipping

into the boxing glove   still hot from my brother's hand –

no way to know the stranger part   of a man two fists thick

    with quarter-worn knuckles   inside red and black

gloves to protect what?   each swing harder   dizzy

still   on the ground   sweltering blood   and trust in my mouth

(Beneath) I Watch One Constellation

When the boy pulled on the strap of the purse
I struggled to take back, I glimpsed a sadness
in his eyes before he let go more than gave
it up, let it come ripped back to me

and kept running. In that split moment, I sensed a key-
hole into something caging his exhaustion (did I, could I
see it?). As I gave the purse I had taken
back to the woman I loved, there was a pain,

a bridge we refused to believe. Uniform-blue hands forced
pressure points, years later, and worked my clenched
shoulders down to the concrete. I felt like a ghost
of that boy. Rage, grief—I wonder if he would feel so

(but I felt so)—flared across me just as instinct
reminds my body: yours is not the time to weep.

The Great Dismal Swamp

We were born in here. With this kindling I hold, dry crumble
from the wind of my mouth, I make a cradle
of these made-criminal hands: black, escaped, free, native, rare

white, sweat-riddled ghosts, sacrifice
secreted along abandoned canals. Find me, find us,
hidden, cleaved to low high ground surrounded
in sulfur gas, elemental. Noxious freedom, a broken stone

hammer, catgut: gifts, from ancestors by your laws not our
ancestors but we need all they chose and did not
choose to leave. Born in here. Slow muscle, belief

in the shrewd heron, mute peat, nameless rodent,
delirious cicada, the poisonous, the gangrene-swollen

paw, and these living hands, and the guilty mercy
of any god mired between here, lower
ground, and impossible ocean. Echoing death

is a kind of survival. Worn down, we are thankful;
those who hunt us end always raptured
in mosquito gospel. Commit to memory the quieted
hate, what punctures the enveloped body: one grown human

given over before the morning, but after we witnessed blood
turn slicker than forgetfulness, branch shards buoyant inside
the wooden dark. Caught in trees, living unbearable angles. Go

back where you came from white man, contract, bloodhound,
we'll camp in the grease-mud, the humid underside of silence.

Wherein I am

mostly in my palms
      shoved deep in pockets
            full of red

dirt and tattered psalms pressed into skin
      inside a threaded edge
          around my waist
   stricken
            strained

     *

   a greased piston
        of a vehicle   passing

the asphalt beneath
     the driver's hand
      slipping

    from the wheel
       succumbing to sleep

     *

confined to a theatre fearing
      bullets on repeat
            watching every motion

picture I was supposed to watch
           only years too late

      with acetate film meant to protect
         my pupils
          translucent
dripping
              anxious blue

          *

      beetle-backed
        exo-
           and gossamer-winged
     spreading
open until too far
      until torn down the middle
          until clouded
             viscera splaying
       exposed

*

moonlight extended

over an open

field in southern Illinois

its southing

I am also

sheathed in green

nearby

and each husk

shimmering in white light

St. Trigger

I'm idolized   I'm   backhanded eye

        taboo   backward

            who holds you   in myself

    close like fire   I'm split   heat spilt

                                  from human   ripped

        thing   but   void and nova   loosed

I'm no   I'm wire   I'm scar

        new   to you   contrived

            cloaked   I'm   antennae

    soaked   wind   looped—   meant to be

        in   anti-antidote   transmitted

            hole   in hope   slewed

I'm end   of obsolescent sex   marked man   music—

        pressed   beneath   ruthless

    I'm   a ready finger   I'm admission and a ready thumb—

delicious decision

derision   religioned

ambitious suspicion   attended

I'm hum   what happens

and tick   doubled   hymn   symptom   I'm rabid

unclocked time   and boom   devoured   face-stricken

lobbed brick   daemoned   born

look   I'm   divided

spewed into   Pantocrator   ashamed

the truth   I'm   aped—

man-i-fold masque

of angels   afraid   fate-taken

I'm debt   ache   I'm   aimed

made   and want   ace

burn   and doubt adept

I'm learned

I've had it

I'm sum

I'm

Rich

rich (→) **adj. 1.** Having abundant possessions and especially material wealth: As in, standing a breath between each other, she didn't realize how *rich* she was until she saw him weigh her past in his eyes. **2. a.** Having great worth or value: Remnants of his mother's voice echoed beneath their praise, inside his spine: we may have enough but we ain't *rich*, at least not like them; don't forget your hands are broken mirrors, how they splinter money-colored clouds. **b.** Made of or containing valuable materials: It wasn't their new world's prospects that changed them: they'd become *rich* with what they'd lost, and because of what they were losing; you could tell by the way it swayed their frames, curved their minds. **3.** Magnificently impressive, sumptuous: Despite the flitting birds of his new money and tongue, his deftly rearranging mind, it was true she was the *rich* one; he forced himself to keep his gaze above the ground, open on her eyes. **4. a.** Vivid and deep in color: They were the *rich* amber of dark honey unbecoming itself in green tea. **b.** Full and mellow in tone and quality: She only hesitates because the stir of his voice feels *rich* as music at the edge of her body, *rich* enough to coax home a ghost. **c.** Having a strong fragrance: Her *rich* scent carries something with it, or in it, not only her but something coming through her, running. **5.** Highly productive or remunerative: Their gods said, what you share won't make you *rich*; what will you do with the coin of your lives? **6. a.** Having abundant plant nutrients: They buried their gods in *rich* soil, then searched for months on hands and knees for warmth radiating from the surface, eager to reap the unwild. **b.** Highly seasoned, fatty, oily, or sweet: Their myths, their histories, their pleas, their systems of conviction and logic; they were too *rich* to not be poison. **c.** High in the combustible component: As in, beyond their own *rich* bodies, they could sense a hiss coming low, too, from their world, willing to explode. **d.** High in any component: So they grew, or swelled, guilt-*rich*, shame-*rich*, and ever-teetering at the cusp of knowing so. **7.** Highly varied, developed, or complex: It was the simultaneous intimacy and distance, the real and unreal sense of their lives, their relationships, their auspices that felt so *rich*: so profoundly yet elusively interwoven. **8. a.** Entertaining; also: laughable: But there is something *rich* here; even – or especially – for them, bearing witness to the near emptiness, the falling. **b.** Meaningful, significant: As in, something *rich* enough to let slip less and less slowly. **c.** Lush: She said, you understand, the same way a certain, pluraled pain is *rich*. Yes, he added, or a certain pluraled crisis. **9.** Pure or nearly pure: Though they thought they were they were not *rich* enough to go.

These Miles

and our neighborhoods, our paths, our eager hands were glass
we couldn't or didn't bother to break. The jagged hold of being

brought-through, unbelonging. Talking to—touching you, we were
made of contradiction. We held the rock salt-eaten pieces, each self
evidence of loss and end. The money we had triggered us

to spend ourselves on lust and fear and trust. Cut wheels, each
choice, precarious above potholes and off-white ice; we braced

for the next fragile season and chance to lie
to ourselves, to whom we loved, too
afraid to not speed up—

we wanted clearer lessons. I am what was taken from me

and I am what was given back
in loose language, loose dollars, loose

comfort—the burn fresh in all of us. I reach out despite

inertia: too struck to tell you I need the rush of touch and take
what's in your pockets for a love just the same.

Manmade Shelter Beneath Rupturing Sky

I can't tell you, but you feel it the way you feel
thunder. The way it speaks rain and beckons
a turning back to manmade shelter beneath

a rupturing sky, a silent *please* between
men who work to claim each other, blood,
who are supposed to take, to prove, to dig wide

around what burns and not speak out
loud about love. Fumes fuse when we hide
words under eaves like bushels of wheat
and watch the barn burn down

as the rain picks up too late. Boys burn down
and aim to take the town with them. Flames flick light
into pummeling rain, billow black smoke when they break

open the cans of tractor grease. You won't let yourself
look away from the burning shed as the structure tears
down in pieces of cindered darkness in the middle
of the storm in the middle of the night.

On Acquiescence

Of Bronze – and Blaze...

We were crossing town again, on the bus. Our point guard who
could never sit still, be stilled, said, *Playin' with my money is like playin'*
with my emotions, between his teeth. He leaned into the aisle
mimicking Big Worm's anger we'd watched on TV. My teammate
and I shared more than the same name. All of us slapped seats

with laughter, barely understanding, on the bus crossing town in ties
and slacks, heading to our JV game. After school but before
the match, I had wanted to say, *don't play* to a girl I smiled with
too much in her white on white volleyball knee-highs and skin,
down in the empty, late afterschool classroom, both of us too

borderline, looking at each other as if lost in the angles of blinds
and skin and dusk. I was never quite sure about her touch, metal-detecting
fingertips seeking shrapnel. We held something quiet. We crossed town,
off the bus. Chins up, another contest, away. Rarely smiling. Undressing

and changing into uniform I remembered her hands, put mine where
she put hers on my body. A boy said, *And you know this, man.* We laughed
and talked shit when what we wanted to do was understand. I remember
the fists of the boy with my name when he, hotheaded and light-
skinned, cut across the court, breakneck toward the white

man hurling slurs from the front row of his home
game, 4th quarter, seeing a tall, blonde son – maybe his –
knocked onto hardwood. The perennial black versus white school
rivalry. When my name streaked towards the bleachers, reached

for the screaming white man, our black feathers rustled
like midnight peacocks claiming our cage, the polished floor.
We were cross town. We were off the bus. We weren't safe.
Not while playing away or sweat-soaked inside
patent leather Jordan's, toes clenched like talons, cursing

with our bodies under the buzzer's horn, straining to empty
what gets stuck in hands, weapons that clutch torsos and throats
hummed in muscle, flexed shut. Off at this distance, I hold less
noise and more silence. But what if we are made of this violence?

Vestigia

The trees teach me how to break and keep on living. Patience
and nuance and another kind of strength. That kind of life
wrought from water and mineral iron and loss, the perpetual loss
that emanates from underneath tongues, leaves. The hush splayed
across the jungle made of memory. More fearful for its lack
of movement. The sad lusciousness our eyes reason from a world
on pause. Motionless green. What we touch and see, immediate
as steam, then gone, collected. Tense, wet beads full of secrets; how
to make a branch long. Nothing swaying the weight of the trees.

2
draped and standing

On Disembodiment

I begin to count what I do to myself each morning:

The naked black man breathes heavily on screen, but
says nothing. His body's expression feels voyageless and
working myself I cannot see his face as the two

smiling naked white women climb determined all over him,
make a boat and anchor of his body. I am touching
myself but I don't know what else I'm doing. I do know

two kinds of annihilation. You know, you want to love—make—
make yourself love a delicious god whose crown is a throne,
its emptiness, no thorns. The exotic is our horizon. Its power

a place for longing, so violent. I want a home. I want a body. More
of my own—I don't want to be a surface possessed anymore. Let me
be one breath needling inside. I know something of what we name

pain, but what part of it, me, precisely, is doing the dying?

St. Seduction

Eros eating my eyes, full-mouth rosy
    smile ever so slightly   righteous—
drooling. I do with my myths what they do
    with me. I do not believe.   I choose to eat
my way through dark   bridges. I swallow
    idle gods. Yours? Whose? They dance
they sex they hand they look they gut
    whatever whoever: all and only
to distort   the way I stilt and syncopate
    through time's violence. Distinguish me
from night   that lives inside you.
    The myth: of me. The want   to want
to be. Wanted. Sacred. Silent. Magnetic—how
    so hollowed by light. Maze of
body. Wracked with pulse and touch. Curve
    and arc and eye. Again. Quick. Smile.
The guilt of whom   I—we—you aren't
    throbbing. I spy the wild bedrooms in bodies
porous with instinct. Smell. Orgiastic loss
    grasps—conspires. The ache
of expiration—exploration. Look. At me
    through them in us, restless foot dangling
off the curb over the puddle into the glance
    of the other—there—upside down inside

you falling. Up. Rushing where with whom and why
        ecstatic and hazed   delicious light   caught
lost falling. Loot   loot—Look through
        into—my face is not a door my face
is not a door my face my—   as if the truth were
        most important. And it, I, too, seduce
as easily as warm sea rising, higher
        by the hour. I do not believe
in righteousness. Such lonely power.

Between

bliss and fear. I learn the waves before

the tides. My wary toes skim
the bottom. What I do remember is
her farther out, in

the bigger waves and her body held

beyond, above my head in the swell—
the inrushing water, for a moment
a silhouette, a threat, sleek, dissolving. Nearly

bodiless, riding, rising—turquoise light,
that is what the guilt is like.

Where We Choose to Hide

It was   absolute. It was gorgeous.   *Stay.*

But gorgeous. Trust. The cold   bending. The light
from the cathedral. Snow in   our lies. The frost—

seething. Slowly, slowly into summer. How we were

              wrongheaded and heavy with music:
its strange weight. Pulsing, heart-like.

Loss-like. The brutal conviction of seasons.
Blunt nakedness.   Sweat-lush

5100 blocks south.   Dusk-swept, swallowed in
skyline. If not   a horizon. *We can't—*

your eyes. Lake dark, wide
                              windows left open

to dying daylight.   Humid light. Foolish light.
11 floors up.   Weeping.   *Trust. Trust*

this.   We still don't.   Give
a secret to a being. Each

collapsed. Complete. Fever made   of touch.

[American Dream] See

two black people [what] in an alley naked
[am i] having sex frantic in a cop car
with the cop lights chaotic [silent?] circling
across the walls [what]. See two black

people in an alley naked having
sex in a cop car cop lights writ frantic [am i]
across the walls [gone]. The sirens fracture
shadows, whir, near – unsilent [?] – drawn.

To whom——to what——do I belong

The mind in night spreads out like fireflies—impatient
lilting over flooding water, nowhere to land now
that they can see, each makes me still look back.

Who reached?—I wanted to be the fateless
cave where someone, you, could lose the world, slip down
its drowsed mind, spread like night around impatient fireflies—

What has my life been laced with?
Needles, threats, amphetamines, insides skitter and pound
though they see nothing. I look away and in and back

and forth, what pulls or lulls or lies stagnant
floods and anchors all I am. Stone sure, I am an edge. Now
night becomes my mind, moondark, impatient, looses fireflies

in this broken trickle through what won't remain, this pit
an open mouth, a living hole, breathing in the end out
more than taking in, like eyes I've watched, like where I look

and hate to look at. Faith, let me be rootless, fluent
as pain and change-slick water. I am you and falling through
darkness in my mind, soft spill of dying fireflies, impatient
in this body, this brink, scheme, see: in here I can't look back.

Interstate

I'm interested in the woman of color working
at this gas station in the middle-of-nowhere Illinois.
The middle of nowhere for someone like me, who
won't ever know her, who won't ever see into the middle
of this place I'm standing. There is something about
how she holds what looks like her exhaustion, how
she is barely elevated behind glass in Shell red,

the only other brown body I've seen driving north and east
in an evening's hours. Her eyes. How she doesn't look at me.
To be alive and black surrounded by such isolated white
is now an antique brutality, a traditional form
of American chaos. I know there must be more
beautiful complication here, that I will always only see
what I want and don't want to see. A different alone,

I'm beginning to believe what I am. Here: there are remnants
of idle names and newcomers and dying,
like everywhere I could ever go. Our hands touch when
she slides change down into a metal gully, into mine.
The hurt is slow. It's time for me to forget, but I only replace
what is happening to us with a loneliness
that moves through, that keeps me going.

St. Who

Who is not callous, not cattle
moving in sequence, a cataract of time,
of blue-grained lusciousness
a green scythe illumined in moon—
who is not night corkscrewed,   not chrysalis tearing into
what we will call heavy in an eye.

Who is not moon moving
in sequence clobbered by time   blue or grain heavy
green lusciousness—   or night scythed   a cataract
of cattle illumined in corkscrews,   chrysalises
tearing into what
we will   call callousness.

Who is not blue and heavy with time
moving in sequence   mooned
or green grain cattled
amongst scattered chrysalises   corkscrewed into
night called will   scythed, called   lusciousness tearing,
illumined, called   what we will.

Who is not lusciousness corkscrewed
in time,   cattle scattered,
a sequence scythed, illumined   like grain

clobbered in moonblue, called a heavy chrysalis
of will, a cataract, tearing
green night, calloused,   you and I.

Through

through (→) **prep. 1.** In one side and out the opposite or another side of: As in, after days of wandering, they finally carved a path *through* the deep woods; the littlest of them all couldn't help but stare at how the standing water had soaked *through* his socks. When he opened his mouth to speak, the bigger ones looked right *through* him and continued forward toward the cave's mouth. **2.** Among or between; in the midst of: She watched him gently as he fell *through* his mind. They chose silence because the sound of their fear travelled so clumsily *through* darkness. **3.** By way of: *Through* sex, they spilled loss and time. *Through* sex, they learned to desire their most intimate disguises. **4. a.** By the means or agency of: She learned how to distinguish between different kinds of smiles *through* her trips to the general store with her mother, grandmother, and later on *through* her daughter. **b.** Into and out of the handling, care, processing, modification, or consideration of: They shuffled his application *through* the unemployment office at the same speed he went *through* each job. His stint on the steamboat casino was his favorite; he remembered the first moment the chips no longer felt like money; the way colors began to blur, passing *through* his hands like the gray chaos of river water. **5.** Here and there in; around: He was sure there was something else speaking *through* his veins besides blood. As they walked *through* the antebellum home, he couldn't believe the way the smells forced their way *through* his clothes, his skin, his nostrils; the staining scent of cigar, the musk of sweat and shame, the lingering hints of salt pork, sweet corn, and gun powder. **6.** From the beginning to the end of: *Through* it all, he had known deep down that he had never wanted to be there. He wasn't sure why he stayed *through* the rumblings and *through* the shatter; why didn't he just say he had to go? He lay there *through* the night; eyes open, mouth closed.**7.** At or to the end of; done or finished with, especially successfully: They were relieved to be *through* each phase of pain. They were *through* with every claim except exhaustion. **8.** Up to and including: They went *through* the first eleven pages of the manifest without finding his name and he watched the man's eyes as he scanned *through* the last one. She had gone *through* all her options; there appeared to be no way out. **9.** Past and without stopping for: For years, they touched and moved smoothly *through* only the bodies they didn't love; together they devised a plan and plot to get *through* the smaller deaths and desires. **10.** Because of; on account of: She thought she could manage to survive *through* silence. He was sure that he could survive long enough *through* some combination of his grip and his feet.

Bridge Named Chain of Rocks

barely above the water : the want running   up the river sick with resurrection
scars   bleeding into memory   my kin and me are you and your

kin till humid soil   sought across centuries of sex shipwrecks and psalms : hum
as you sink   your hands in the sink with chipped enamel plates and iron ballasts

cannons pickling jars copper ingots nematodes freshwater sharks   and captured silver
platters tarnished gray as the day now gone : hum your hurt like the hog's head

with the fat radish arranged   in his static mouth : call this pain   a crooked end
dammed   a delta ever-writhing sin-slick : bright eels like fingers needling

the upper river unremembered   unlit and splintered : wooden barrels and their makers
hung and hanged   below a black dome awash   in wet reflections : Mississippi

mud in moonlight   in Missouri or Minneapolis or Iowa as easily as Vicksburg or
Ostrica when you hum cracked   lips warm and billow boats of human

steam into the contours of history's face : colder than the shards of locust left
in winter battered open : the blind surface of northern ocean : hum

the hurt the stone   open   swallow the to and fro : swallow the crossing
the tug of the unquiet the undercurrent   low and heavy : stair   vein   song

Sta. Soledad

Especie de dios, que no me toques donde me queda
     The crescent ache that meets the light
     And blinds my failing eyes that work
Crisis, aun voluptuosa, en contra de cada cuchilla de momento,
cada década de
     Desire tumbled down, ripe with what I won't admit I love

     Each prayer of breath and touch sliced open not enough
Cuando nos dejamos extinguidos, más torcidos que juntos, pero así fieles
     To the black hole heart not greedy not lonely
     Only doing what it is supposed to do: claiming
Como la material que somos, hinchada con Gracia, llena del fin tanto
como lo abierto

Her Song a Cliff a Cage

How did it end up in that house. Hand-forged
burl and bole and shoulder. Figure sheathed
beneath cloth. What sunk and became
the room. What was draped and standing

taller than this woman who made the woman
who made me known. Restless wire sacrament.
A hole made of music comes wide, inhuman from
a crooked instrument, a torso almost hollowed,
rimmed in shades of pink and ivory. Nothing

black about this anchor. Beyond memory, she touched
its strings, spilled improbable sound. I will
always be a child to that harp. Confused.
Never allowed to touch. A deafening gleam when
its music moved through lightless rooms, through

walls and bodies alike. I became silence. I've become
cumbersome as love I cannot hold. Then let me be
that music that consumes midnight. Let me make
chords with what comes from this blood.

Do you prefer answers or truth?

what if you don't
believe that bodies hold
anything they say they do

and what if you're a belief
and little else? maybe myth
remains like embers, blood,

electric flesh life-lit –
but if it isn't, then you aren't
holy, only a quiet

know how to be
home – a chosen risk
makes a perimeter

barely believed in? what
pulses and courses
within any sluicing heart

still embodying the dark
wavering mind, muted fire
breathing space, between

a root buried in time or
haunting inside belief – and
around the death of love

conjures depth, shapes
the barriers of memories,
but your body is more than

pyrotechnics and scars –
then you can't be, won't be
all impossibility holds

46

Meramec (Cavern, River, and Ironclad)

Watch the ice melting
in the glass: togetherness.
Our throats stay open: we
swallow. On the dingy carpet
floor, heat high, we winter-

sweat. If I tell you a tragic history
you believe me. But when
I talk about us, race—you're
dumbfounded. Incredulous.

The ruin here to you is not
credible. But I escape down
into it while you fall beside
me. No: This was a dim bedroom.
Scent plus intoxication. This

was my verge, a shard of anger
fighting crying. This was you coming
toward me, me opening the door, leaving
only the room, me hearing you
sobbing. Same mating song I'm

committed to singing. I refuse
to participate anymore. I participate
endlessly. We both dream we wake
up in the middle of sex—we're still here,

asleep. Refuge becomes the frozen porch
when night opens and won't close,
when I can't breathe. I lay my face down
between your legs when I can't stay
hard and fail to convince myself to be—

I'd say you still love it (me when
I do it) anyway. I never know ruin
until I become it, fall into—I can't climb
up. Not down. Not now. I'd do anything
for you to listen—No, I wouldn't. See—

Too Far North

in the copse: the sanctuary's fretwork breaks, burns,
abandoned, up through the ends of stars. I name each
forest Today and Why and Year and Gone. Blamed
because I trust the wolf, the owl, the cliff, the lip of rock
above the vulture that murmurs *look*. I counted. I took.
I wove myself in with the leaves. My fortune did not
surprise me. Thought, then forgetfulness—what if

I believe fear is its own low country? I follow
an hour behind an hour and the tower inside
an elegy. I am anybody helpless, listless, near
as whisper, as prayer. There is a stillness inside every
valley and door. I build hundreds of my own angels
and dare the cold to mold me daily into a bridge
between what I have forgotten and what I owe.

St. Window

Not what can I touch, but what can I hold? This never
really felt like home. This street never could have
belonged to me. I retrace it with my body, breathe

the distance and cold I've known. The heavy sound
of geese moving aches perpetual and native within me:
dark streaks, out of sight, not song. I am a compass

the shape of my grandfather's mouth. I watch his
sudden rasped breathing, how it scares me, makes me
thankful when its lull transforms, becomes a seam

across both of our bodies, wanting to gather,
to close. I approach. What I am ripples outward
when I reach the brink of him. There must be a brink

where green crags lit black with condors sweep down
in impossible angles, trajectories, cusps between
us. We watch age to learn what's coming. Life

guttural and frantic in this dailyness, this unforgiving
lifting. I begin to touch a living body gently
desperate, convinced I do not know my own.

3
of sudden roots

Very Many Hands

I sit twelve people down the church pew from you, burning to catch the rhythm in your blinking. I seek more than your face. It hurts to see the way sound makes a tunnel. Its root-veined walls there then gone. You and I compose another kind.

***

Witness my long line of lovestruck liars: those who can't take the sky, deceivers of their own eyes, change lovers, receivers of forgetfulness, ecstatic touchmongers, merciless collagists, the spiritually jackknifed, ever-children and the like. I am each of them and heavy hands red on cold glass holding why-still-blue water, in dull music, surrounded by bloom, fear-lit and forever-fraught. This is a truth; not-quite-closed eyes scrambling over nakedness elusive as hope. But barely hope. Lovestruck, lying, I wonder about everything I'll find in this body. And this body. I wonder what it knows. I wonder about yours.

Brushing against your hand, pale, at the Ohio River

Invisible memorial for me. Its facelessness worn present
with your guilt and my grief. I will always doubt

what you can hold, what you can see. My face gives, takes
in late sun on slow lines, gossamer rites of spider web

high up in trees: I know a loneliness in our desire
that became shame—your face comes close, but never

here. Living things hold loose gatherings in the night
branches the swaying height of a dead man above me.

My hands escape yours to touch the trunks of trees. When
did I choose not to believe? We can't hold what

you won't witness, confess. We don't survive. I hate
not myself but this returning sightlessness surrounding

as it keeps us separate, a distance we conceive.

On Communication, 1880

The new telephone
lines and poles stood between trees.
Soon, it happened. Here,

again. Rope, then bodies strewn—
same old ingenuity,

     same innocence, killing me.

Elegy for Apogee

Drowning? Consider this: What is desire? Who or what devours
what or whom? How close is absurdity, is irrelevance, is danger?
In denial? In the divine? In dilated eyes? In sunken hands

scrubbing pans in the kitchen that cooks hunger beneath fish-
greased dish water? What is that tremble in the feet and the mouth
of the fly romancing the crumbs on the brim of the sink

from the night before? Do we have to eat everything? Do we have to
chew endlessly and never burn our tongues or choke
gobbling soup or razor-thin hidden bones? This deliciousness

still too hot? Too piercing to the throat? Can you choke her
if she asks you to squeeze hard no harder no keep going but don't
enjoy it too much? Do we have to lust for nights fucking fucking

otherness until we hear the clink of new armor gleaming
sweat-polished and mooned by breath turned noise? Can we lie
there in our sex exhausted and breathe and swallow and remain

touched, halved, conscious of conscience? Who prays to St. Doubt? Whose
conscience? Whose collateral? Whose collapse? Who loves the end? Who's
dark as the id? Breed the id? Eat the id? Be exotic to myself? Enjoy

the translation of my body in whose mouth? Who can make
work the hurt and urge and rage like words, like puzzles,
like a body, but whose? Bring out which tantalizing beings

from the stockroom and wild reserve of my own? Pile platters high
with meat and cheese cultured and aged in the skin of a what? Cut it
how? Watch for what to gush? Spread it how? How much of this mind

is mine? Where is my canary? Who has the brand new one-size fits-all
jumpsuit and boots, the helmet with its dim light barely carrying?
And what should we do with the soot seeping into the porous

pornography of my taboo-being giving up? Who owns the other
wild canaries kidnapped from their islands for cages of coal-
fraught mines? Who can explain what happened? Dondé

estaban? Y dondé estoy? Como vas ahora negrito? Negrita? Como
andas adentro conquistador sin doors? What did you ever love enough
to try to take, to force open, to touch, conquistador? Disfrutas de deseo

tanto como dices? Do you hate as much as you say you hate?
What about the tired yellow disappearing from all these
delicate feathers? How long do we have to wait

to coat our quills with kindling before we explode? Forget
my ancestral antique cave? Forget my myths? Forget my holes?
What about the spilling-in cold? Where's the hair? Where's the bulk?

Who's been shorn? I am on display as owned bones in what museum-
made-home? What want won't leave me alone? Why and how
do we fuck and war, pattern and rattle the windows in the ecstatic

upper rooms of the special collections gallery? Who can say they love
the ache of their anger? Who can really say they trust their anger
the way they trust their want? Who doesn't ask? Who's anxious? Who's

anchored to the brutal arc inside of eyes? To drunk fumbling hands
atop the antique dining room table? To the loll of heirloom lace? To felt
green worn corners on whose pool table? To the sacrosanct crawl

space? To the bare hangers clattering in whose closet? To the craters
in the body's moonscape movie set backed by big time producers of what
screen-stitched nostalgia? To which actors delivering breakthrough after

breakthrough performance after performance? To which decrepit theater
of my body, collapsed and taken back by the roots and vines of trees,
an abandoned stage, dim and splintered now, with what kind of want?

After

I lock a foreign door behind me, leave her
     sleeping. Three days wordless and now
I will not see her more. Her. And will never see

You. *By and by*. We: fragments of you. And I am made
     by loss. I may never love, hear, and know

the child with the mind I had before. You were us. Now,
     I am made older. Here: Dimly lit

exits and entrances, muted corridors cut
     through an end inside, spiraled blood and dark—
I know a quiet, but don't know who or what

     you were, I am, was. I slowly break a giant
lotus the color of rain cloud with my mouth; stray

     petals, forgiveness, saliva
inept along my lips. Echoes: a shrill woman breaks

     her voice over my body, scowls before she pleads
with the walls I've cobbled into me. A young, tall preacher
     in his prime smiles, mouth closed, and

places faceless coins
      in the deep palm
of my left hand. The bent wire

      grip of the lantern I don't want
creaks sharp in my other hand, thin glass lets go

      tattered streams of light, ill sway, insignificance,
absence, beneath raw white sky. This snarl of intuition,
      a clutch of sudden roots, believes,

but does not speak. What I remember is everything, but
      I know that can't be.

On Sustenance, Distance, Sky

Winter countryside like a broken circuit board;
patchwork frost and the irregular meld

of shallow shapes made heavy with blue burns over
ice covered ponds. It may take too much to see inside

the aching mouth of the bass banished, surviving, trapped
by winter in the low. But I want to see the end of living sinew

move beneath the ice fisherman's hands, to see inside the dark
space he saves for recollection, to witness the pace and depth

of death, and what makes death, to see who I claim to be heaved
into the unreal sky like plumes of smoke. From a distance,

barely violence. I can't scratch the lovelessness that
remains flagrant in my eyes. I only want to understand

the hole beneath the grief. I only want
to cover this blue-lit world with clouds.

I. ALL WAYS, THEY TAKE MY CHILDREN I contrive to tell
you what I know you know. I wonder about what I can't tell you
openly—and why. Make games, play lies accordingly. I am afraid.
Everything about this world screams fear of fever. The old ones
put their ears to the ground. They wait. They get a sense of what
is coming and how to know when to go. I read what masters keep
secret, speak to you of eggs and butter and blue clouds. Hear
underneath speech and we will see what comes of this war, what
will will come down like gravity, down to this South.

II. IN THE REBEL'S DIN I am not the only contraband. I may
be a different region of the sky—may one day cover us. Those who
see the blue or men beyond the woods run for one or both. These
trees between worlds no longer hold the secrets where we used to
meet. The old ones aren't all ready to let them go. Let the trees go.
Let the secrets go. I can't let this skin go. I don't want to bloodlet
home, go.

III. THE FATHER GENE In each movement, through the world, I taught myself a new I. I can love what is not yet and will become. Discarded I's fall slowly from my life like family. I stay put because I trust no home. I leave because I trust no home. Loving, I am believed to be— sick outside my body. Outside my mind. Sickness taught me love. Sickness taught this I to see— to see what dying slowly brings. I trust what remains in my eyes more. I am moon-white. I almost died. I was always almost dying.

IV. TOM FORGIVES My own release would never be enough. I'd die for a cause because I don't believe we dying. Blue better be better than gray, I tell you. Afraid to eat, I'm so hungry. My throat is full of low country. I ain't hiding. Least not no more. This name Tom is barely mine. My name means no tomorrow. Can't you see me? See? Least let me see you over to who hides in the open.

V. NON-DREAM Don't you dare tell me a thing you think I don't know about me – about us. I know the doctor wants to plumb my fever. I know you're all feverish with fear of fire. I know. When I sing I hem fire. The hypocrite is eager. I refuse to kiss your fingers. Each day I forget again what was want. I'm wound and bandage. I'm known and unknown. Sold seven times in six weeks, they say. My skin whispers my blood's confessing. Your eyes – like my eyes used to, way back when – let me hide in the open. Now my eyes open.

VI. MORAL WARHORSE Make me cymbal. Make my brass turn blue. Future, I'm you. A little less fever and a little more war in my veins and gut. I would not shoot my former owner. I shot your former owner. Call me honor, not horror, out in the open. They killed Tom but not tomorrow. I still miss my Mama. So I need to be a hero. Must be. I'm blood-slow riot. I'm regiment. I'm soon-to-come religion. I'm road.

VII. THE FATHER CRIME Go back in time. Tell about the ones not ancient and not alive. Tell who lied. Pray, tell. European deities, barely belonging to each other, are restless, reckless, and aim to taste the Mississippi. Love, now. Change, now. Lie, now. Need. Hide the blood from the children. Love, keep the children in the dark—no, in the light in the plea that breeds the secret.

VIII. WHITE SHADOW Stay back, in time. Careful, cousin, lies are beautiful music. Black music. Believe me, cousin. Our land does not agree. Our law, our land. Choose wisely what you will call your country. We are not amused. We are full, so made more eager. I see you see where lies belong. You need not ask for what you already grasp, you own. This is only our home.

IX. GIVEN WHOLE Children, present in time. Notions made of time. Skin signatures. Blood thinks. Don't say difference is sin sickening my mind. My mind wars like a country. We diddle like countries. Flee what you can of this fervor. Remember, I never knew a home. The body's constitution is immythical, is unpeculiar. And yet, this Peculiar Institution. Your lips bury mine. Cover yours. Forever inside what I once owned.

X. INHERITENCE Dear Cousin, I never lied. I will take. I will make mine. I will spend your children. I will make them honey or make them wine. Now I'm horizon line. Some will learn to die. Some will learn to fight. But this war, ancient? This war is just another and more fever.

XI . A M E R I C A N   C I V I L I T Y
Outside the body: We are two different people. We are too different
people. We are two different people. Inside the body: We are
two different people. We are too different people. We are two
different people. We are too—   We do not believe in one.

XII. SPOIL Now, war over,
they say this is my body. I
had to go to see my former
owner. She did not know
how not to be my owner. I
showed her. She will always
be a miss to me. Where are
the old ones that remained?
Do they remember me?
What will they make of my
blue-uniform being? Do they
still meet between the jagged
trees, with secrets?

XIII. VOID You and I are searching for two different people. We will find and fall into Revival in a dark wood made of me, made for me. We bore into family. Our losses love each other. Your mother, my grandmother. Don't scare her. I am a violent dawn beyond my body. Can I not hide? I want to find what you found in the wood.

XIV. ECHO FOR GROUND Body between fear and faith, I make a kind of freedom. I make medicine with my mind. I find the things I need. I find and make and leave a long kind of family. No seeds have been given to me. I am not quite haven. I still need to run. I river up and down this country. I am eager. I break inside of night. Still, I.

St. Doubt

Long abandoned T-beams
make darker broken angles in
the night. I'm only walking.

After stillness, I look again.

In death I am as many as the rain.

You think you can, but you can't
forget the burning fingers
of the sun. Can't release each way
you've been touched.

I watch one boy
concentrate on malice:

he skateboards hard, leg cocking
the wet snow's air, underneath
an orange wool cap. Eminem blaring from

I don't know where. Winter is
native to him. Us.

What I've found here is killing me.

The way they moved on
asphalt brought tears through my body.

I lay down
intestines in the place of my throat.
I lay down short breath in the place of morning.

It feels later than it is. Your laughter
sounds like bare feet in mud,
but to me it only speaks *please*. Show me

the rood, the roots and veins
of your ugliness. (Let me

taste.) This sadness is
yours. I am nothing but
the moving dark—

You say *believe what they have*
already when I say *I want*
to give my language to the trees.

I don't want that forgiveness.

Amen. If it is so. Thank god
I am not one of them.

4
risk a bridge

Very Many Hands

I am wrapped in a shawl of patchwork wants. Of languages displaced in veins. Of sheet rock cut open with explosives to force through byways and sow man-high seas of crops, to make space for interstates, for cold emergencies and tanks, and touch.

***

Which ballast will sink, loose, explode? Which myth expires first? If it's true what you remember, that my laugh billows like a man you loved who lived before my life, then whose is my body? Whose memory lives inside my body? Whose sluice box? Whose wharf? Whose cleared forest? Whose slow-failing factory monotony? Tell me more about this body. Tell me its smoke doesn't dissipate on cue, minute, inscrutable. Tell me how pollution pollinates fire. Show me what floods this Middle West quicker than water.

***

I am stitched together with the risk inside Desire. Call risk a bridge. Call one palm full of why-still-blue water—oh, how my mind is just my mind crossing. Not the limb of a ghost stuck in the hinge of a door. Not the fight lost inherent in a child. Who was it that dipped her index finger into my mouth, fished that penny from my tongue, saved me from some dumb Desire? Who was it? Who watched as I stood there too in line, too silent, trying to fall behind, an almost question in my near-new eyes?

On Surrender

The soft dark rope of prayer and dream,
its weight, what I pull, and am pulled by
into night. Crude apparatus. I walked into what seemed
to be a wake in the ordering line

of a 24-hour McDonald's downtown. I was camouflage
contraband, everything I looked at looked back
black and white. From my peripheral, I witnessed

my counterfeit life: the only police
officer I've ever trusted, an ex-lover,
a savior, a martyr, a brother, all there

waiting: worldless, anxious, hungry—so many leaned
their shadows on each other. Someone I knew once
spoke aloud to no one: Who broke me open?

The nightwind and what it carried made it hard
to know. Time was a threat we noticed so
I gave in to slow sex that felt like a memory,
got zip-tied by that police officer, then haphazardly
released. I never got my food.

                                White people
I vaguely recognized talked shit about Detroit
comfortable between the cramped
bathroom's piss and stone and I felt
myself swell to defend a city within
whose limits I've never lived. I'm ashamed
I don't trust anger. I'm ashamed I don't trust
the idea of home. Outside, I saw the war

                                              aging again. I wanted
to sit on the floor, sit until I was served, and eat, but I knew
nothing, no one, would come. Until too late, our bodies
couldn't grasp the incoming weary glory of the out-of-date
military drones, gunning at us, until they were less
than the height of an abandoned tenement above
the ground tattered with violence, spitting up
crumbles. Before anything else: the numbness

of this danger, this power. We pushed
each other into the parking lot's narrow
sorrow and threw hand-size chunks of rock

into the sky, and hated the way the child-like
among us paused in awe of the destruction.

You are less if you miss, we'd say. *Keep fucking throwing.*
Each one of us, on our own, gave up. I went back

inside to find someone I still love. The two of us rushed
to stash our bodies together in condiment cupboards
beneath the cash register. We made ourselves pray
but my knees wouldn't bend enough

to close the little door, so I left her there. Went back again
and pressed my hand on the glass
exit, took in the sudden emptiness, and felt the toll
stir my body, full, with no need for hope.

God's Island

Then a man is a place;
a room cluttered full of walls
within walls, wants within
wants, windows within
gaunt mirrors and more
mirrors long and home
enough with hidden sharpness
to catch and reflect each
and every act without seeing,
without making even
the slightest shattering sound.

Struck at the Benefit Ball

The beloved has become a collage at the edge of my body

along with this blind music spilling
from what into what was
once nowhere.
           Forever asks: is
to begin better or to end? Could you
call death the debt of consciousness? Or only my own
precious difference?—and
another: what is safe and not
lost in the undertow of my coin moon-
pulled mind? I don't always want
to claim, to call this
mine. This for-a-moment slightly swollen

           lightless heart. With no need
        for light. Sobered then seduced by
what our bodies do with time—this love

secretly loves to be indebted to it
        and pleasure—Finally: is it
              fever? Is it never sickness?

St. Casualty

So I'm sitting on the train just looking at you and I'm mostly sure you're looking at me and through
the chaos at my edge I clench I watch Fear looking over at one of us. As if through the false window
of a strayed mirror's angle. You think back, say Why'd you fucking do that? I don't use words to try

to answer. But now I see you see despair like glass breaking. And Fear's staring. Heavy. Sure, I begin
a specific posture. There is a repartee between bodies; bright pain streaks through the fragile ritual

of ours. Fear knows its own. Finally I say I did it because I was anxious long enough and what is
the real difference between deception and—dying? We can't go back. Talk was a bouquet, regret

we handpicked, shame running from our faces. We can't—it's done. You're done. Gone. Don't give me gone. But you wanted gone didn't you? Now, open as night I begin to catch how we collect

the gravity of Fear's eyes. I don't know where I'm getting off so I'm holding my body out vaguely in
an effort to hide. You don't quite look like you're following. You might do something violent. Or

you might just go. Love. We do everything but wait. We've already fucked up—too many strayed
angels and catastrophic nothings. So when I rip the glare from inside the night's rhythm my blind

harbor and make it tear the air I see your and all the other riders' necks unnerve with something
more brutal than choice—I only turned its terror on me then because I'd sworn I'd paused too long
(you can fall from any height) looking past Fear's smokewhite teeth, its mouth my halo my hive.

If We Were Sacrifice

Sound never finds its center, but
if when I come I pronounce *I sing*
the body electric with slow intention
out over you grasping slipping forward
out over the back of the broken futon,

[so this is you—
so you want—]

completely indulging in myself after having
played between you with my lips from late-
late night to early morning not just
to appease you then what will you have
known about me, about us and what

[so this
is what you
want. so
this is what
you want]

will we become? *Mad filaments* plied
delirious, our curious love-like touch—
The violet sheet and tattered mattress

creak full with scattered collusion
scattered half-light and offering bodies

[so this is what
you want. so
this is what you]

open to want to see not mind not watch
confusion. A clear blue *sprawl and*
fullness leaving the hands done roving.

[*You linger*]

St. Accessory

Night. My face open over the closed eyes
of the sleeping I. Witness—a way made. A Nyx-
bloomed narcissus. Wet mouth desperate
inches from a world shuttering, exposing,
taking and changing. I'm—I've forgotten
each way and reason why this I's forgotten
me and what it means to sleep or be
awake. I stumble forever through
the seedy house of my birth still
dreaming up the fallows of what
happened to me. Chords swollen yellow
and white with jonquil sin and song I won't
remember the way the scream the shame
the whisper plumed thick as fog. The work of
my body hidden in a gnarled trunk;
a wooden clock not yet carved,
still, uneasy in a tree. I is a device. I is
a choice. Tattered book left open
by wind. Shunted mouth where the creek runs
high. I am *remember when?* Moon-stripped
and gaunt, your fuse and home. Long-headed,
krill-swarmed like the boy toeing the bayou
in your grandmother's dream. Kiss me.

But the Myth is Too Beautiful

A man made gone, a violence. I caught myself leaning

in a garden full of fragments: violet, brown-black, red-grey

      and what was with me, in me, while I did not know

slowed: something nearly dead, a gun begetting rust, jagged pearls of sunlight

    and the naked ghost to whom I reached, far across the garden, the cinder

blocks and raw concrete, the broken avenue, the sewer drain, the live trees, the old wide

windows and the old wide doors inside the distance

     between us, some locked, some unlocked. I saw I was still an animal

and would always be one, confused beneath shades of comfort and want,

    berserk with something beyond the idea of love. No one looking

saw what I was. I sliced open the idea of blood. Realized time is whole

     and I will never know it—its brutal stillness, how even

it changes. In the glimpse, I stopped. I came apart

    like ritual song in a child's mouth, like grief inside a life.

It is not a question of memory

Frost, inexplicable in a mirror like a river
muting my reflection, I see trembling
southern fields, clouds clotted with
shine. Body, still wet, covered
in cold, where the South hides. I
run water over fear, a descant
for recollection. A slow drip down
this nose, lips, chin, down, through
the shoal of impulse and each
border of this torso, scar-laced hip,
belly, thigh, shin. Beneath. My South
thick with pulse. I'll flux into
history, but first let me fuse
language, anguish, touch; give me time
to settle with what anchors shadow
to this face this morning. My South:
both gulf and border, black highways
stitched and caked with rock salt,
the corpse of a red-tailed hawk, swollen
then frozen in ice, now mid-thaw
in the cattails, a sandbar eclipsed in
the stench of sulfur, and my remaining
barefoot in autumn on a man-made
beach, Lake Michigan, even after the wind

picks up. A dozen monarch butterflies
strewn like candy wrappers in seaweed
washed ashore, somehow so close
to asphalt and fluorescence; an iron
city's core. My stark hand damp,
tracing the warped wooden door, South
still staring back through the asking
mirror, back through the memory
of a trip South I've never taken before.

Black Objector in the Soldiers' Chapel

Louisiana, 1951

Young and coveted and given
tacit dominion. Her words forced more
distance, barely touched him; he was
kneeling, rising now. She said, *we don't pray like that
down here.* Eyes learn how to know: half-
lit, contemptuous as night bloomed
like a bruise beyond wrong clouds. Teach
one man his difference. Teach one woman disdain
for her desire. Sunk in sin, sanctified: I am
my imagination: familiar with a phantom

limb that reaches out to try to clench
a nameless weight we press into a place that haunts
like recollection. Resurrection. Forbidden, unforgotten
skeins of syllables took shape and sprang from his
hard mouth and thousands of miles and hours
that begat days that begat this, my body, a deafening
clock made opaque, tragic as being a consequence.
What else. He said, *The way she shamed my God, I knew
I wasn't—I was far from—I wasn't
anywhere close to home anymore.*

Notes

The epigraph quotes Ida speaking to Vivaldo in James Baldwin's novel, *Another Country*.

"Rich" and "Through" were inspired by the dictionary form of several poems in A. Van Jordan's collection *M-A-C-N-O-L-I-A*.

"The Great Dismal Swamp" takes its title from a large marshland area in the Coastal Plain Region, encompassing southeastern Virginia and northeastern North Carolina. The area was said to have harbored many peoples who fled enslavement and persecution in the 17th and 18th centuries.

Of Bronze - and Blaze..., the epigraph of "On Acquiescence," refers to Emily Dickinson's "Of Bronze – and Blaze." The italicized language in the poem quotes the characters Big Worm and Smokey in the 1995 movie, *Friday*.

"Between bliss and fear", the title and beginning of the first line of "Between", quotes part of a sentence in James Weldon Johnson's *The Auto-biography of an Ex-Colored Man*: "The anticipation produced in me a sensation somewhat between bliss and fear."

"Bridge Named Chain of Rocks" was in various ways inspired by the Chain of Rocks Bridge, which spans the Mississippi River at St. Louis, Missouri.

"Meramec" refers to a large, partially-commercialized cavern in Missouri and to a river in Missouri. Also, the USS Merrimac was a boat seized by the Confederacy and converted into one of the first ironclad ships of its kind. In its first battle, it wreaked havoc on the Union navy before the Union's USS Monitor, an early submarine, fought it to a stalemate. Confederates burned and sank the Merrimac to avoid it being recovered by the Union.

"*Shadows Uplifted*" is a radical translation of Frances E. W. Harper's 1892 novel *Iola Leroy, or, Shadows Uplifted*.

The italicized language in "If We Were Sacrifice" is taken from Walt Whitman's "I Sing the Body Electric."

The title "It is not a question of memory" quotes James Baldwin in his essay "Many Thousands Gone" in his collection of essays *Notes of a Native Son*.

Acknowledgments

I'd like to extend my gratitude and appreciation to the following journals and anthology in which poems in this collection (or earlier versions of them) were first published or are forthcoming:

Apogee, Bettering American Poetry (anthology), Boston Review, Button Poetry, The Cincinnati Review, Fence, The Greensboro Review, The New York Times Magazine, Meridian, Palimpsest, [PANK], Pinwheel, River Styx, Southern Humanities Review, Southern Indiana Review, Third Coast, and *Tupelo Quarterly.*

Also, a number of poems in this collection appear in the chapbook *St. Trigger*, winner of the 2015 Button Poetry Prize and published in October, 2016.

I feel such deep gratitude for and responsibility toward all the challenging, inspiring communities that made this collection possible: To my parents and my family, thank you for continuing to teach and support me through your love, grace, and complications. To my GBC boys, we are our anchor. Diane Seuss, thank you, eternally, for your manifold guidance, for showing me what courage is and can be. Mary Jo Bang, Jericho Brown, and Carl Phillips, for being such powerful, compassionate mentors, for challenging the work and challenging me.

I offer my thanks and appreciation to the communities of the Creative Writing Program, Comparative Literature Program, and the Chancellor's Graduate Fellowship Program at Washington University in St. Louis for their unique and essential support: social, emotional, and financial. Thank you to Cave Canem, for our faith, resilience, what we're building, and how we're growing. In addition to those named above, I would be remiss without extending special thanks to Espelencia Baptiste, VersAnnette Blackman-Bosia, rebecca brown, Kathryn Davis, Timothy Donnelly, Danielle Dutton, Kathleen Finneran, Rav Grewal-Kok, Saskia Hamilton, Kathryn A. Hindenlang, francine j. harris, Jennifer Kronovet, Paul Legault, Liz London, Miriam Martínez, Philip Matthews, William J. Maxwell, Charleen McClure, Sope Oyelaran, Mithil Pandhi, Vivian Pollak, Katie Prout, Katherine Simóne Reynolds, Martha Rhodes, Claudia Rankine, Justin Phillip Reed, Line Rindvig, Mónica de la Torre, Phillip B. Williams,

Eileen Wilson-Oyelaran, Rafia Zafar, and Pablo Zavala. Thank you, too, to all the other friends and artists, too many to name here (I see you), that have offered insights and encouragement along the way.

I will always be grateful to the communities of educators, writers, and young people in Madrid, Spain, Durban, South Africa, and Chicago, Illinois, whose influences will resonate with me as long as I am. Thank you to the Fulbright Program, the Beeler Fellowship at Kalamazoo College, and Literature for All of Us, respectively, for their financial support in those endeavors.

And always: thank you, Andrea, for the person you are; this path with you feels sacred.

Publication of this book was made possible by grants and donations. We are also grateful to those individuals who participated in our 2017 Build a Book Program:

Anonymous (6), Evan Archer, Sally Ball, Jan Bender-Zanoni, Zeke Berman, Kristina Bicher, Laurel Blossom, Carol Blum, Betsy Bonner, Mary Brancaccio, Lee Briccetti, Deirdre Brill, Anthony Cappo, Carla & Steven Carlson, Caroline Carlson, Stephanie Chang, Tina Chang, Liza Charlesworth, Maxwell Dana, Machi Davis, Marjorie Deninger, Lukas Fauset, Monica Ferrell, Emily Flitter, Jennifer Franklin, Martha Webster & Robert Fuentes, Chuck Gillett, Dorothy Goldman, Dr. Lauri Grossman, Naomi Guttman & Jonathan Mead, Steven Haas, Mary Heilner, Hermann Hesse, Deming Holleran, Nathaniel Hutner, Janet Jackson, Christopher Kempf, David Lee, Jen Levitt, Howard Levy, Owen Lewis, Paul Lisicky, Sara London & Dean Albarelli, David Long, Katie Longofono, Cynthia Lowen, Ralph & Mary Ann Lowen, Donna Masini, Louise Mathias, Catherine McArthur, Nathan McClain, Gregory McDonald, Britt Melewski, Kamilah Moon, Carolyn Murdoch, Rebecca & Daniel Okrent, Tracey Orick, Zachary Pace, Gregory Pardlo, Allyson Paty, Marcia & Chris Pelletiere, Taylor Pitts, Eileen Pollack, Barbara Preminger, Kevin Prufer, Vinode Ramgopal, Martha Rhodes, Peter & Jill Schireson, Roni & Richard Schotter, Soraya Shalforoosh, Peggy Shinner, James Snyder & Krista Fragos, Megan Staffel, Alice St. Claire-Long, Robin Taylor, Marjorie & Lew Tesser, Boris Thomas, Judith Thurman, Susan Walton, Calvin Wei, Abby Wender, Bill Wenthe, Allison Benis White, Elizabeth Whittlesey, Hao Wu, Monica Youn, and Leah Zander.